Do You Know What I'm Thinking

A Collection of Poems & Short Stories from the Modern Man

Guillaume Valcourt

Library of Congress Cataloging – in- Publication Data has been applied for.

Book Publishing Services by Pen Legacy LLC.
Cover by Christian Cuan
Editing & Formatting by Carla M. Dean, U Can Mark My Word

Paperback ISBN: 979-8-9880702-5-2

PRINTED IN THE UNITED STATES OF AMERICA.

FIRST EDITION

Table of Contents

Do You Know What I'm Thinking

A Collection of Poems &
Short Stories from the Modern Man

Something Beautiful
I Found in You

I remember the night we met.

I can still envision the outfit you wore.

Dressed in all white,

You were such a beautiful sight.

From the moment of your entrance, I was in a trance.

As I watched you, I knew I had to ask for a dance.

If I didn't, I would miss the opportunity to meet someone—

Someone as beautiful as you. So, I took my chance.

As I nervously approached,

You looked at me and took my hand.

I wondered and pondered on where this would lead.

In that moment, all I knew is I found something beautiful in you.

Guillaume Valcourt

Now that the song has ended and I'm no longer in your arms,

I am gone and just a distant memory.

But remember this poem and the moment we shared,

Because something beautiful I found in you.

I still think of you many nights on that dance floor.

In that moment of time, you blessed me with a dance.

Because of it, something beautiful I found in you.

And it is something beautiful I will never forget.

The Number 13

Allow me to awaken and enlighten your conscious mind, as I bind and dispel the superstition, misinterpretation, and fear with the misrepresentation of 13—the number, to be exact.

Let's go back and track the truth, displacing the roots of this myth as you ascend your conscious mind to find the truth to this numerical transformation and its true manifestation.

Let's begin from the start, first from within.

13—the traditional age a child becomes an adult, going through rites of passage. Bar mitzvah, 1st holy communion, and tribal rites are performed on the 13th year of birth—the age of puberty, the beginning of the menstrual cycle, and the transformation of the physical body to maturity.

The number 13 represents a new beginning—ascension and raising—not demise as we've been led to believe and perceive. Realigning our vision and gaze with our truest state. Aligning your vision and gaze, allowing the spirit of fear and ignorance to keep our minds from the truth.

Let's take a trip through history and point out some signs that are hidden to some but wide open to others.

Jesus plus 12 disciples = 13

There are 13 tribes of Israel (*Num. 1:20-47*):

1. **Reuben**

2. **Simeon**

3. **Gad**

4. **Judah**

5. **Issachar**

6. **Zebulun**

7. **Ephraim**

8. **Manasseh**

9. Benjamin

10. Dan

11. Asher

12. Naphtali

13. Levi

Coincidentally, the United States was founded and fought for its independence with 13 colonies:

1. Virginia

2. Massachusetts

3. Rhode Island

4. Connecticut

5. New Hampshire

6. New York

7. New Jersey

8. Pennsylvania

9. Delaware

10. Maryland

11. North Carolina

12. South Carolina

13. Georgia

The 13th Amendment ratified and gave slaves freedom under the Constitution. There is one judge and 12 jury members in court proceedings, equaling 13.

There are 13 zodiac constellations:

1. Capricorn

2. Aquarius

3. Pisces

4. Aries

5. Taurus

6. Gemini

7. Cancer

8. Leo

9. Virgo

10. Libra

11. Scorpio

12. Sagittarius

13. Ophiuchus – the Serpent Holder, which the sun also passes through

Do You Know What I'm Thinking?

There are 13 moons in the calendar year.

Metatron's Cube has 13 circles, the basic creation pattern of existence. The pattern of thirteen independent circles (female) is one of the holiest, most sacred forms on Earth, the FRUIT OF LIFE, and is hidden within the lines (male), connecting all the centers of the circles.

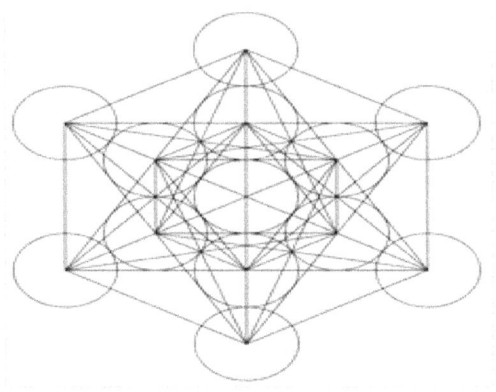

13 is the number reflected in all patterns of life. It can be seen in man, nature, and the heavens. It is transformation and ascension—evolution to a new beginning, continuing the cycle of life. Fear it no more, but embrace its power within you—the number 13, which represents transformation.

Guillaume Valcourt

A Warrior's Way

To be ready at a moment's notice, facing opposition and challenges without hesitation or reservations, fighting for self-preservation. Displaced from home and loved ones for months and years at a time, I embraced the battlefield as my mistress with cruel intent.

Pent-up anxiety upon returning home to strangers who no longer recognize me. Damn, I don't even recognize myself. Masking the tears, fears, and pain compiled from battles on the field and in my mind as I try to find peace from the demons that bind this tortured soul and mind of mine.

To the brink of self-destruction and malfunction. Plagued by nightmares and flashes of past experiences. Feeling alone despite being in the presence of everyone. Finding solace and comfort in discomfort 'cause chaos seems more rational for desensitized minds finding peace and solace in a hostile environment.

Uniting together to battle multiple foes building and forging a bond, longing for the day and time to return home to a simpler time. Until then, a Warrior's Way is my path.

Guillaume Valcourt

Father 2 Daughters

Be aware of those who come in the night

To lead you away from what is right.

Deception and misconception are the tools of their trade,

Trying to bed you down so they can get paid.

I've prayed on my knees over both of you

On those nights when you were sound asleep.

I prayed our Lord and Savior would give you insight

And guidance on the things I could not meet.

When you're both grown, up and off on your own,

Discovering what life has to offer,

Remember the foundation that was built at home—

Love, Faith, and Hope.

Do You Know What I'm Thinking?

Deception and misconception will come in many forms.

Trust the Lord and your intuition, for it will always know.

Believe in yourself when others don't believe in you.

Your self-belief will be your source of strength.

Remember, nothing successful is ever done alone.

Remember to dance to your own beat.

The melody you create no one else can repeat.

It's sweet like honeydew and soft like the morning dew.

Like mana from Heaven floating down, there I will be with

eyes Above, continually watching over you.

Last, my daughters, be sure of what you want in yourself.

It will be the beacon that attracts others to you.

Be wise in the love you choose,

Making sure they are worthy of the gift you give.

Don't fall for the physical because it's the internal beauty that

rises above all…

Character, integrity, and the ability to love and forgive.

These words are from a father to his daughters.

Love always, Daddy.

Guillaume Valcourt

Algo Hermoso Que Encontré En Ti

Poem - Something I Found in You (in Español)

Recuerdo que esa noche te conocí, te visten de blanco y lo que es un Bellamente sitio.

Usted me tenía en un trance, el momento que la bailar, yo sabía que tenía que tener una oportunidad como la marcha por la noche o perder la oportunidad de conocer a alguien alguna vez Bellamente como tú.

Así que me acerco a usted un neverous todos los que le solicitará que tienen un baile, medida que tomó mi mano me pregunto y reflexionar sobre este se iría yo no lo sabía, pero me encontré con algo bello en ti, yo heridor y reflexionar sobre si eran más jóvenes que nosotros han sido amantes o amigos o

18

que he sido un extraño? De cualquier forma estoy contento de que tuvo una oportunidad ... Porque algo Bellamente que encontré en ti ...

Pasar muchas noches abrazándote fuertemente en mis brazos como la luz del sol me despierta con usted en mis brazos, a simple vista una y nos vemos en la paz y siguen siendo motivo de dormir algo Bellamente que he encontrado en ti .... sabiendo que nuestro tiempo llegará a su fin, pero cada uno de los momentos con ustedes me siento tranquilizado a medida que crecemos de desconocidos para los amantes y compartir esos momentos de placer me lleva más cerca a ustedes. Porque algo Bellamente que se encuentran en ti.

Cuando me haya ido y ya no en tus brazos recordar este poema y los momentos que compartimos algo Bellamente porque he encontrado en ti. Nunca te olvidaré.

Guillaume Valcourt

Carrying My Heavy Rucksack

With the weight of the world on my back,

I trek thru this life with my rucksack.

The platoon leader says double-time.

Damn, I feel the pain coursing thru my mind,

And my body burns…

As I carry my heavy rucksack on my back.

Expectations of me seem unattainable,

Standards set by others without my buy-in.

You're an officer now who is expected to know to hide your

Emotions and move on, soldier.

Duty calls…

As I carry my heavy rucksack on my back.

Do You Know What I'm Thinking?

I ponder as I stare up at the heavens, awaiting a sign from the
Universal grand architect on the course of action I should follow
for the choices, decisions, and responsibilities I bare alone...
As I carry my heavy rucksack on my back.

Plagued with trials and tribulations, I maintain composure,
Putting my faith in those things unseen or not heard.
To the outside world, I look strong in stature and in control...
As I carry my heavy rucksack on my back.

But, internally, I battle my demons and fears every day.
My tattered armor is damaged from past battle campaigns,
Present-day wars, and the fights yet to come.
Still, I carry my heavy rucksack on my back.

I long for those days of peace and comfort,
When I am no longer tormented.
But until then, I will continue with the cracks, dents, and
Imperfections on my withered frame and mind...

Guillaume Valcourt

As I carry my heavy rucksack on my back,

While waiting for my next battle and call to duty.

Yesterday To Today

Yesterday, I was immature and young—

Short-sighted in my views and thinking.

I saw what I thought was the big picture,

Not realizing it was only a distorted image of my

perception… 'Cause yesterday, I was young.

Yesterday, I had all the answers.

'Cause in my mind the world was simple…

One-dimensional…

Straightforward…

Blinded to the complexity of situations around me.

I judged people's actions because that was my reaction.

'Cause yesterday, I was young.

Guillaume Valcourt

Yesterday, I was innocent about life's expectations,

Feeling untouchable to life's ebbs and flows, highs and lows.

'Cause I only saw the innocent, young things

My young mind would allow me to see.

'Cause yesterday, I was young.

My yesterdays have turned into today.

I can see clearer and further than yesterday.

'Cause today, I'm a lil' bit older and somewhat wiser.

Today, I'm no longer innocent to life's ebbs and flows,

Highs and lows. Instead, I'm a vigilant watcher of all her tides.

'Cause today, I'm a lil' bit older and somewhat wiser.

I dispense more of my senses today

So that I won't misinterpret the message.

I look beyond what my eyes permit me to see,

Hear more than the sounds my ears allow,

Smell past what my nose picks up,

Taste every flavor and ingredient,

Do You Know What I'm Thinking?

And feel beyond the touch of my fingertips

To the depths of my soul

'Cause today, I'm a lil' bit older and somewhat wiser.

Today is a new day that is about to finish.

It's made to be cherished 'cause it wasn't promised to me,

While teaching me to take advantage of your gifts and blessings.

Someone is always in need of your gifts and blessings,

Even the ones you think aren't of value to you.

Those tend to be the ones that are of true value to others.

Today is about to end, and tomorrow is on its way.

I'll remember the things from yesterday to today

To take me through tomorrow,

So as I get a lil' bit older and wiser, I can pass it along.

'Cause tomorrow, I'll be much older and just a bit wiser.

Guillaume Valcourt

Reflection

I ponder about my life's deeds and wonder how will I be seen after I'm long gone, remembering the highs and lows like the ocean tide with its currents that ebb and flow from the moon's beckoning pull.

Blowing her breath like the winds of time erasing my accomplishments and debris of failures, I tend to contemplate and debate on this road and journey I've had to take— sometimes choosing decisions to make with no clear road map or direction to take.

Being guided and directed by minds and thoughts of other's past mistakes and emotional tides, I parade thru this maze of life like a thief in the night hoping to find that light, but all too often getting caught up and lost.

Do You Know What I'm Thinking?

Still, I keep moving and trying to figure out my way thru the struggles and doubts of life's charade and strive to build my faith, but not without a price to pay. 'Cause anything desired and wanted has a price, they say. The heavy burden that I bear alone and the voice that continues to speak to me…

From HIS THRONE whispering to me:

"Keep Going On, My Son,

For it is within U to

Achieve ALL U

Desire and Want.

And know that

The road you travel

Is narrow but necessary,

For from it, it will build in U

Character!"

Guillaume Valcourt

Can't Get You Out of My Mind

Can't get you out of my mind.

Visions of you keep running through my mind all the time.

My mind is stuck on you, refusing to let go.

Like a child in a candy store, I want more.

Green light says go, but my heart says no.

I lose my composure at the slightest thought of you

As you pull up closer in my rearview mirror.

What should I do? What will I do?

Damn.

Can't get you out of my mind.

Visions of you keep running through my mind all the time.

Do You Know What I'm Thinking?

What you did to me, causing me to stumble and succumb before I Could see what was coming at me, you FINE BROWN THANG!

Can't get you out of my mind.
Visions of you keep running through my mind all the time.
So, I find myself putting together these letters into words, words into phrases, phrases into sentences, and sentences into this poem to convey my thoughts, feelings, & expressions for you.

I keep rethinking why did I succumb to you.
Was it the look in your eyes?
Or was it the things you said that swayed me to stay?
Caught up in the current of emotional feelings that are so strong, I was swept away and ready to say...I lay down my heart and soul to you because of the joy you showed me.

Can't get you out of my mind.
Visions of you keep running through my mind all the time.
I knew it wasn't meant to be.

Guillaume Valcourt

But I wouldn't be real if I didn't chase my dreams,

No matter how impossible it may have seemed.

Still, I can't get you out of my mind.

Pleasing Her

Meeting in a moment in time, exchanging names and numbers with subtle pleasantries and a smile. Communicating and chatting often for long periods, and eventually going out on a date or two. Drawing closer to one another until that day when the subdued thoughts and feelings come to life. No longer able to deny what's been long overdue.

Our eyes meet as she takes my hands and places them on her breasts. I feel her nipples rise from the sensual caressing pleasure I'm giving her. I begin to gently suck, each suckling becoming stronger and more intense… 'Cause pleasing her is my thing!

She closes her eyes, letting go and clinching my head to her breasts, giving me full control 'cause she knows this is will be the best. Grabbing me harder and tighter to express her pleasurable enjoyment of what we've just begun, she moans while saying my name, wanting more and more of this Pleasurable Principle. To feel me inside of her is what she seeks, and I'm more than obligated to give her all of me. However, it is with a slight hesitation because I don't want this to end quick… 'Cause pleasing her is my thing!

Me loving her, pleasing her, and making her weak to her knees is so irresistible that I can't resist. I pull her closer, feeling the warmth of her body next to mine. The sweet aroma of her essence, perspiring and trickling down her legs, sends chills all over my body and causes my nature to rise. As I feel her heart beat faster and faster, I know now it's time… 'Cause pleasing her is my thing!

As I explore her body with sensual kisses, I eventually settle in between her thighs where that luscious valley lies, harvesting her fertile grounds with my tongue as a sickle… 'Cause pleasing her is my thing!

Do You Know What I'm Thinking?

She moans in ecstasy from my lick and suckling of her clit as she screams, telling me not to quit and to keep up the pace. As I suck her clit, her love spreads all over my face... 'Cause pleasing her is my thing!

Her legs began to tighten and quiver, letting me know she was about to erupt. Despite her multiple orgasms, I continue like a captain of the ship as she tries to pull away, screaming no more can she take. Still, I fight to maintain my grip on her clit as I make her cum over and over and over again... 'Cause pleasing her is my thing!

When she's weak and drained from releasing her sweet treats, I release my grip and dip myself inside her so she can feel my arousal deep within her... 'Cause pleasing her is my thing!

Ever so deep inside her, I feel her pulsating and throbbing, or is that me? Nevertheless, it feels so good, her squeezing her muscles tighter on me and locking her legs around my waist to handle all of me... 'Cause pleasing her is my thing!

My strokes begin slowly with every other one quicker and stronger than before until her lock is broken from the pleasurable force of my strokes. She moans in pleasure while holding me and telling me to keep it coming… 'Cause pleasing her is my thing!

Our eyes lock in the moment of ecstasy. As we gaze at each other, she gasps with pleasure. I take that as my cue to flip her over and proceed from the back as she toots her ass up and curves her back, inviting me all the way in. I part her cheeks like the Red Sea, ready to slip it deep within just how she likes it… 'Cause pleasing her is my thing!

Each stroke gets stronger and stronger, breaking her down. Our bodies are no strangers to this feeling of pleasure—me inside of her and her feeling me, touching her walls as she moans, begs, and screams… 'Cause pleasing her is my thing!

As I feel myself ready to explode, I hold her tight by the waist to ensure she feels all I have to give. Cumming so hard, it leaves her filled, but it's not the end. Just give me a minute or two, and we can go again… 'Cause pleasing her is my thing!

Guillaume Valcourt

Genocide Black

They say I am part of a lost generation destined to plague this nation—cold, heartless, and only driven by anger that feeds my rage.

Born to the streets, raised by the streets, educated by the streets to be killed in the streets. Their lives, full of potential and promise, are often compromised by misguided decisions. They ignore the signs that keep them from falling and lead them to demise, living for the moment without room for direction or reflection.

They say they are an endangered species, a ticking timebomb full of rage, set up for failure, and targeted by the government for economic genocide instituted at birth to prepare them for a cheap labor force at PEN U, where they go as a rite of passage to develop and hone their craft. Or is it the other way around to perpetuate that generational curse?

Their only legacy left behind is their illegitimate seeds. Too young to be a dad, but it's the fad. Damn, what am I to do? A father at fifteen with three strikes—Black, Young, and Male.

They pose with pants hanging down, identifying their form of coolness misunderstood by elders who don't realize it's a form of defense for survival and acceptance. The cooler you are, the more respect you get.

Their world revolves around a four-block radius, scared to leave the hood 'cause it's a refuge. The old heads on the block are the teachers who show love and school them on the hard-knock life when no one else does. They hug their block 'cause it's their entire world. Scared to chase that American dream, they create their version of it. Now ignorance and anger are their throne.

While they kill each other off day by day, the blood of the innocent cry out. Unknowingly, they are helping Uncle Sam complete his task of the genocide of the Black male through his seeds.

I Got The Fever

I GOT THE FEVER!

Never did I think it would happen to me.

Damn, I got the fever.

How could I get this incurable disease?

Damn, I got the fever.

Thoughts and ideas rush through my head.

I'm trying to figure out how I got misled.

Damn, I got the fever.

I can't stop it from spreading each day that goes by.

Damn, I got the fever.

Never again will I underestimate its power.

Damn, I got the fever.

Guillaume Valcourt

My immune system is down, and now I got the fever.

The writing bug has caught up with me.

Shame on you for having naughty thoughts…

About the bug that you thought I caught.

Damn, I got the fever.

My Heroes Are Black

Long before there was a man able to leap tall buildings in a single bound, run faster than the speed of light, and fly through the sky…MY HEROES were Black.

Long before they scattered them across the ocean, dropped them off here and there, spreading my descendants across the four corners of the world…MY HEROES were Black.

Long before she journeyed through the Underground Railroad, risking her life for others to taste the winds of freedom…MY HEROES were Black.

Long before they treated them like second-class citizens, and they fought and died only to be treated less than equal, saying they came from gorillas, apes, and baboons, and calling them coons…MY HEROES were Black.

Long before they discovered the pyramids and tried to claim them as theirs, attempting to rob us of our own historical identity and put their face on the stamp...MY HEROES were Black.

Long before they were saying, "I'm BLACK, and I'm proud," throwing a black clenched fist up in the air, showing solidarity and chanting songs like "We Shall Overcome," and revitalizing the Black conscious mind...MY HEROES were Black.

Long before they claimed us to be a threat and met us with opposition, titling us Public Enemy #1, beginning the irradiation of a mass group of people...My HEROES were Black.

Long before John Hanson was taken out of American *His* story and the two-dollar bill as the first black President of the Continental United States...My HEROES were Black.

Do You Know What I'm Thinking?

Long before they sailed the Seven Seas, rediscovering what was already seen and explored by the original one by way of the Canaries Current, which joins with the North Equatorial Current off the Coast of Africa to connect to South America…My HEROES were Black.

Long before they rose against the masters, being the first to gain independence while guided by Toussaint Louverture, Jean-Jacques Dessalines, and others (sac pasa, Haiti)…My HEROES were Black.

You see, my heroes are Black 'cause they look like me. I'm a decedent of those who are royalty, prophets, great thinkers, builders of nations, educational university inventors, navigators of both the seas and stars, sciences, geometry, astronomy, and people of a mystic mind and conscious thoughts. They remind me to always draw from their strength so others can draw from me.

I'll never forget that my HEROES are Black.

Observation of Life

Life is the greatest teacher, as some say. Unfortunately, like many of us, we didn't pay attention when instructions were given in class and therefore ended up retaking the "course." This time, we take the "course" while focusing on what is at hand. In my observations, I have come to realize some things, such as the power of the mind, are truly amazing. The mind becomes what it sees and hears. When it sees and positively hears things, it responds positively. And just the opposite, when it sees and hears things negatively, it responds negatively.

People fail in life due to ignorance (failure to know), superstitious (lack of belief), and fear of taking a risk. We often try to compartmentalize people into categories, missing the real lesson and purpose. The age-old questions are asked: *Why are we here? What is our purpose in life?* I say we are here to love, fellowship, and help out our fellow man. Everyone has been through something that someone else is going through now. Life is the teacher of self. What you learn or don't learn from life is what you discover or don't discover about yourself.

Guillaume Valcourt

Pass It On

This is a word from a dad to his son.

The dad talks about the right and wrongs he's done.

In these words, he imparts his heart

So that it may become a part

Of his son to pass along

When he becomes a dad and writes his own "Dad to Son."

These words are a guide on what could and should be done

When challenges come.

Do not run, for it is within you to overcome.

Trust in our God, for He is within you and your spirit.

You are a creator, and your reality is what you say it is.

I know you'll be great and strong

Because you've heard my words and seen me create…my SON.

Love Always, Dad

Rage
An Urban City Teacher's Perspective

Rage! Why are we angry? We're frustrated working in an environment where we are understaffed, underpaid, and overworked. They say it's for the kids, but is it really?

Dilemmas arise every day, brushed aside so we can make it through the day. Uncontrolled anger, suffering, and pain scream out at us daily as we walk through the hallways. It's sometimes a wonder how we manage to take ourselves out of the situation and refocus on the cause without even receiving an applause.

Clock in early and leave out late. They say we are family, but what about mine? When it's all said and done, it's about THE BOTTOM LINE. The annual estimated revenue generated is astounding, which explains their growth from one state to six states and growing within a five-year span. They're building these schools faster than they can man them, leaving casualties of staff along the way.

The company man says you need thick skin and a high tolerance level to deal with this group. *Which one are they talking about?* I sometimes wonder about the bureaucrat players that say what you want to hear but do what you don't want them to do behind your back, or the students who are hip to the game and think they can do it all by themselves.

It seems like we are just pawns in the matrix, made to believe in something that really isn't and wondering when will we wake up.

Stolen Legacy

My HISTORY, vague and unknown, scattered across the four corners of the earth by the hands of the Occidental Man.

HIS-tory recreated to make us out to be less of a man and an abomination of the races that was their plan—scheming and plotting against our HISTORY.

Looted from us in the darkness and stolen by the Occidental Man, our HISTORY, rich and strong, is a legacy to the Original Ones— the Black man—who withstood the manipulation of that man's hand who banded against us. Yet, we still overcome and overstand all as one.

Our HISTORY—diluted and molested—was stolen along the span of time and retold to the blinded masses. Open your eyes to see the obvious—that the key to the future is reclaiming our past and seeing the light that once shown so BRIGHT.

Our HISTORY plagiarized by those to make HIS-tory, but our HISTORY is no mystery no more, reclaiming the truth to our self, minute by minute, day by day, year by year. Cutting to the roots of their lies to relink back to our own True Man (Mind, Body, and Soul), moving us to a higher ground where our minds aren't locked down or hands tied down.

Although 500 years have passed since the first Europeans landed on my Motherland, where their plot began to transform our HISTORY to HIS-tory, we are waking up and building our bond with one another, moving in one accord.

Once, Black was viewed as good and positive. It's even been scientifically proven that the color black is an absorber of energy. If the laws of nature know the truth, then how long will we be ignorant to the truth of who and what dwells within us?

Do You Know What I'm Thinking?

For we are like trees planted along the river bank, bearing fruit each season without failing. Their leaves never wither, and in all they do, they prosper...BLACK HISTORY, MY HISTORY.

Guillaume Valcourt

The American
Dream Community

White man is killing the Black man, and the Black man is
killing the other man while kids in the ghetto fall by the
wayside, chasing dreams that seem to have no meaning 'cause
they've been conditioned and programmed to self-destruct.

Hate crimes keep rising. No more is it just White on Black. It's
Black on Black and Brown now. It seems like the whole Civil
Rights Movement just shut down. Or is that what they want
you to perceive? To believe in the propaganda is a trick of the
trade used to parade a lie being played.

Mommas are killing their babies, murdering a generation
'cause they can't cope with the vision of no hope. Or is it the

Do You Know What I'm Thinking?

dope playing tricks on their mind, binding 'em and holding 'em down? The poison makes them unable to find their way back out of desperate times to reality because the Matrix got 'em on that good fix turning tricks—mentally and physically. Me and you, we fail to see ourselves drowning in a sea of sorrow and misery as we keep sipping, dipping, and tripping into darkness.

Sammy pimps the community, causing brothers and sisters to sling, trick, and bang while chasing the American Ghetto Dream, but they are too blind to see the politics behind the industry. The pachyderm and mule have also been playing us for fools, selling us the American Dream that never really included you and me, the Original Ones, but the corporate conglomerate. So, we created our own commerce and business system, only to have them buy us out, force us out, or change the plan because we tapped into their business cash flow. So, they illegalize our form of business and commerce, trying to kill our entrepreneurial spirit and destroy our credit rating along the way.

Guillaume Valcourt

To those who sold out for a shout of fame, never to come back to give back, what a damn shame! And those who did come back only came back to take back from those that lack the means— victimizing our people, stealing their dreams, and leaving them stranded on the roadside of that American Dream. So, I vowed to make a means for others like me who came up through the struggle. We will bind together like strands on a rope, pulling up those who've lost sight of faith and hope or needs that extra lift when no one else believes in you to persevere through the struggle. We got your back.

The Storm

(*Step Pantoum*)

The storm would huff and blow all night.

The storm blew harder as we crossed the meadow.

But it began to whisper sleep to us.

Darkness was coming.

The storm blew harder as we crossed the meadow.

I felt the wind like the storm's heavy breathing.

Darkness was coming.

The flakes hissed and stung our cheeks.

I felt the wind like the storm's heavy breathing.

All through the woods, mice and squirrels bustled about.

The flakes hissed and stung our cheeks.

Leaving snowy footprints.

All through the woods, mice and squirrels bustled about.

But it began to whisper sleep to us.

Leaving snowy footprints.

The storm would huff and blow all night.

Guillaume Valcourt

We're Not Just Gym Staff

To enrich the lives of others' minds, bodies, and souls is our goal.
We're not just gym staff.

It's not only about throwing balls and running around, after all.
We're not just gym staff.

Evolving one's consciousness, raising their level of awareness…
We're not just gym staff.

They think what we do is easy, but there is nothing easy about engaging and disengaging the negative views of a troubled youth and the misconception of an adult mind.
We're not just gym staff.

Neglected and often left out of the equation only to discover the solution to our situation…
We're not just gym staff.

Do You Know What I'm Thinking?

Outsiders looking in think it's sweet but never recognize we move to a different beat.

We're not just gym staff.

We're oftentimes misunderstood because most don't value what we do.

We're not just gym staff.

Our wisdom is as fertile as the banks of the Nile River, flowing on one accord as we unite together.

We're not just gym staff.

As I'm reciting my thoughts and you're listening in awe to the creativity of this poem, you recognize now...

WE'RE NOT JUST GYM STAFF.

Who Am I?

WHO AM I?

I'm that brother running thru your mind when you're laid back chillin' and sipping on your wine.

WHO AM I?

I'm that brother standing in the dark, waiting for you to open up the door to your heart.

WHO AM I?

I'm that forbidden fruit that tempts you to bite. Don't be frightened of past hindsight.

WHO AM I?

I'm Mr. Right, the one you're scared to get with up close and tight 'cause you're waiting for Mr. Wrong to do right.

WHO AM I?

I'm that brother thinking about you day and night, night and day, trying to find my way thru that maze you've made.

Do You Know What I'm Thinking?

WHO AM I?

I'm the blues in your thighs, stimulating your mind, waiting

to erupt at just the right time. Those thoughts go through your

mind as you explore the feelings of pleasure I would give to

you.

WHO AM I?

I'm the one with visions of making love to your mind and soul

before your body even knows the climatic sensual pleasure

that erupts from a touch. Slowly, you feel what I feel,

something real to be sealed by two souls becoming one.

Whether it's right or wrong, I can't deny what burns so strong.

WHO AM I?

Who am I? Who. Am. I?

I am what I am, and that is who I am.

Who I am is a friend and lover to the END.

Guillaume Valcourt

Who Are They For?

(Step Pantoum)

Why can't so many people find a job?

Once you're in prison, there are plenty of jobs.

Who are they for?

If you don't work, they beat you up.

Once you're in prison, there are plenty of jobs.

Prisons are a profitable business.

If you don't work, they beat you up.

More prisons are being built.

Even more are on the drawing board.

Prisons are a profitable business.

Prisons are a part of the government's genocidal war.

More prisons are being built.

Even more are on the drawing board.

They're a way of legally perpetuating slavery.

Do You Know What I'm Thinking?

Prisons are a part of the government's genocidal war.

Who are they for?

They're a way of legally perpetuating slavery.

Who are they for?

Guillaume Valcourt

Will I Be?

Will I still be a man when I'm weak and bleak, unable to compete, defaced by society's many faces and woes with no trace of a man who fell behind the race and could not keep up with the pace to cross the finish line?

Will I still be a man when I can't face my fears and my burdens fall down my face as tears for all the world to see?

Will I still be a man when I've shown you the innermost depths of my soul and heart, imparting you with the key to open up that part that's never been seen? So, I hold on tight for fear of the pain I may receive.

Do You Know What I'm Thinking?

Will I still be a man when I never had a thought or plan to believe in me so I could achieve my dreams and see what I could really be?

Will I still be a man if I've been deceived all my life, led to believe in a false misconception about me and failing to see what I could've, should've, and could potentially be because no one ever told me to believe in my own dreams?

Will I still be a man when I've become a burden to you and unable to continue providing as a MAN should?

Red Sonja

Red Sonja, sleek and beautiful, alluring and dangerous. She prowls through the streets and becomes one with nature, unleashing her power with a simple twist of the wrist—my Honda CBR 929. Perfume of oil sitting up high with pipes sticking out from her backside. Petite in stature, red and black, she's strong enough to hold my frame.

Red Sonja, sleek and beautiful, alluring and dangerous. We've been through a lot, both so close to death. Twisting and turning, becoming one with the road, unleashing her power with a simple twist of the wrist.

Red Sonja, sleek and beautiful, alluring and dangerous. You've not allowed others to sit on your back and feel the

Do You Know What I'm Thinking?

sensation of being one with the road, rolling in the pack and passing onlookers as if they were still.

Red Sonja, sleek and beautiful, alluring and dangerous.
We've had our moments, like getting caught in the rain and avoiding sudden mishaps that would have turned into pain—with the exception of that Sunday when out of nowhere, that truck collided with your body. I thought it was over for us, but the Lord had plans for me.

Red Sonja, sleek and beautiful, alluring and dangerous.
I knew I had to confront my fears and get back on to ride you again. I could not let you sit out in the pasture and fade away with the memories of you and me riding with the winds, becoming one with nature.

Perception

Thoughts and ideas created from visual illusions
of what appears to be but are ignorantly ill-conceived,
perpetuated by a blind narrow mindset to find yourself bound
by what others perceive you to be or not be.

Seeded, bred, and fed by ignorance,
you battle the unforeseen and unheard. The whispers
misunderstanding of you attempting to set it straight or set it
off and show a clear better vision of you, but you back away
scared to say and overwhelmed.

But perception in this hypersensitive culture continues to
deceive the masses who only look with their eyes and fail to
utilize all their five senses as they continue to perpetuate a
false perception and encrypted charter assignation of you.

Do You Know What I'm Thinking?

Perception of thoughts that become words and words that become actions and actions that become habits and habits that become character and charter that becomes your destiny of what someone else's vision and definition is of you.

So who am I to you? What do you see before you? Strength and confidence, or cocky and arrogance? Whatever your ill perception is of me and others that you see is only a small cascade view until you get to know who you are looking at personally and not from a worldview.

Before you perpetuate and create a perception of a one-dimensional view, step back and look again through your lens and see the multi-dimensional layers and the perception you may be giving of yourself.

They say perception is reality, but your perception has nothing to do with my perception of my reality.

Guillaume Valcourt

He Is Me & I Am Him

He is I, and I am Him. We've been conditioned to neglect Him and diminish our true connection only when we need Him in dire situations perpetuated by life's revelations, not realizing that He is I and I am Him. Just not ascending yet the level to recognize that He is I and I am Him—God, Allah, Yaweh, Elohim, and many other names we've given him.

We are blinded and lost because we are taught to look for Him externally, losing sight that he is already internally within us. (Genesis 1:26-27) Let us make Man in our image, in our likeness, and let them rule over the fish of the sea and the fowl in the air, over the livestock over the earth, and over all the creatures that move along the ground. [27] So God created man in his own image, in the image of God he created Him (you and me); male and female He created them.

Do You Know What I'm Thinking?

We are strangers to our true selves, neglecting the Supreme
presence and being within us. He is I and I am Him, waiting
to awaken, ascend, and receive all that's within me. But before
I can see Him that is within me, I must uproot the seeds of
doubt of who I am and embrace that He is I and I am Him, so I
can begin to live in my true Godly manifestation and
experience…because now I know He is I and I am Him for all
Eternity.

Sum of All

She represents the beginning of the birth of a continent and nation, the Sum of All.

She comes in many hues and shapes—Black, Brown, Red, Yellow, caramel, tall, short, curvy, thin, thick, and round. A beautiful and elegant mother of humanity, many have tried to taint her painting as an illusion. But not me. I see you and who you are—half of the Ankh, the key of life.

She represents the beginning and my existence, the birth of contents, civilization, and nations…the Sum of All. She is beauty, for she is the bearer of life. She is strength, for she perseveres thru struggles and strife. She is love, for she nurtures hers and others, bringing forth kings, queens, and warriors. She is the Sum of All.

Do You Know What I'm Thinking?

She is wisdom with purpose that moves about thru the winds of time, teaching us and forming our first thoughts in the world. She is the Sum of All.

I am the key to unlocking her destiny. She is the key to my legacy, intertwining and binding to one another like the Ankh, nurturing and loving. She is the Sum of All and All of Sum.

My being resolves around her. She's the center of my purpose, the purpose of my drive, as I strive to provide and define my life. I think and dream of her in those quiet moments, deep inside my mind where I find my peace and solace where she awaits me.

She is a Queen, Mother, Daughter, Sister, Companion, Lover, Friend, Wife, Life, and Woman. My woman, she represents the birth of humanity, a continent, and nation. She's the Sum of All.

The Message

This message is to us…for us…by us who should trust in us not fuss with us but believe in us and start discussing with us how to stop distrusting us who are just like us, so we can build us up to start trusting us and not allow those who continue to break us up and call it Justus.

This isn't just for us but all of us to start discussing us and stop dissing us who fight for us, causing us to disbelieve in us robbing us of our HISTORY and giving us HIS-tory.

This message isn't just for us but by us and those that seek the lost truth of us. Let the God in us awaken and ascend, and our Lord and Savior continue to bless us, not forsake us in the hands of the ruthless and vicious one who continues to feed on us. Causing us to distrust in us and the trinity power who gave us all righteousness and power to rise above and move us to reunite those who missed us back in with us.

Yes, this message isn't just for us but by us to remind us not to forget us, 'cause we all we got to solve the mysteries about us that revolves around our history, knowledge, and wisdom. Understanding is consciousness within us. Legacy, legacy, let us see will this message wake us and move us to seek the truth that lies in all of us or will all of us just continue to let this pass us by.

Time will tell at the end of the day what they say about us and how much of a difference was made to those of us who didn't let the message just pass us by but took it and gave it to the rest of us.

So, remember this message is to us…for us…by us to entrust to all the rest of us, my people the human race.

Guillaume Valcourt

Will You Let Me Be?

Will you let me be your Mr. Right despite all my imperfections and shortcomings, knowing I may not do or say all the right things? Still, my heart and intentions are with you in mind.

Will you let me be all I told you that I would be despite our barriers from past journeys and relationships? Will you help give birth and offer support to the words and expressions I have for you that will bring you joy?

Will you let me love you when you are weak, lonely, and feel I'm so far away, knowing I'm always just a thought and phone call away?

Do You Know What I'm Thinking?

Will you let me take the journey with you of finding out who you are, as I'm always ever learning, discovering who I am and love?

Will you let me get next to you emotionally, mentally, and physically so that I can see you—all of YOU?

Will you let me be me in all my imperfections and fear not that I won't sway away?

Will you let me be?

Guillaume Valcourt

A Rose in the Desert

Today, I found a rose in the desert with tall, slender stems and prickly thorns drawn toward her beauty and strength. This beautiful desert anomaly piqued my curiosity.

What situation arose that would explain why this rose chose to blossom here? In the harshest conditions, how did this rose overcome its environmental condition, enduring hardships of the heat by day, the loneliness and solitude of cold nights, and the sandy winds and desert storms of turbulence in what seems to be a barren land.

So far from home, this rose I found blooming alone, vibrant, and radiant in this desert dune. *Am I in an oasis or dreaming?* I pondered to myself. I don't think anyone ever told this rose that where she blossoms couldn't and shouldn't be done.

Do You Know What I'm Thinking?

Then again, I suppose that is what made her a beautiful, natural anomaly despite conventional wisdom.

There she was in full bloom—this rose I found in the desert dunes. Time will tell how long this rose will continue to grow there. Will her seeds of life, beauty, and spirit spread across the dunes to duplicate and thrive in the worst conditions? Or will she wither away, leaving me to be the only witness of this beautiful anomaly of a rose that I found in this desert?

I realize this rose represents so much more. It symbolizes **Hope, Strength, Perseverance, Character, Beauty,** and *Insight* for those battling the harsh desert-like conditions of life. The rose I found showed me that we can overcome any situation and condition and rise above false narratives. What I found in reality indeed found me in my time of trial and despair— A ROSE IN THE DESERT.